Listening to **Leaders**

Why Should I Listen to MY PARENTS?

Christine Honders

PowerKiDS press™

NEW YORK

Published in 2020 by The Rosen Publishing Group, Inc.
29 East 21st Street, New York, NY 10010

Editor: Greg Roza
Book Design: Rachel Rising

Photo Credits: Cover (insert) Valua Vitaly/Shutterstock.com; Cover (background) Artazum/Shutterstock.com; p. 5 LightField Studios/Shutterstock.com; p. 7 India Picture/Shutterstock.com; p. 9 Robert Kneschke/Shutterstock.com; p. 11 oliveromg /Shutterstock.com; pp. 13, 19 Monkey Business Images/Shutterstock.com; p. 15 TinnaPong/Shutterstock.com; p. 17 Image Point Fr/Shutterstock.com; p. 21 George Rudy/Shutterstock.com; p. 22 michaeljung/Shutterstock.com.

Cataloging-in-Publication Data

Names: Honders, Christine.
Title: Why should I listen to my parents? / Christine Honders.
Description: New York : PowerKids Press, 2020. | Series: Listening to leaders
Identifiers: ISBN 9781538341681 (pbk.) | ISBN 9781538341704 (library bound) | ISBN 9781538341698 (6 pack)
Subjects: LCSH: Parent and child--Juvenile literature. | Parents--Juvenile literature.
Classification: LCC HQ755.85 H66 2019 | DDC 306.874--dc23

Manufactured in the United States of America

CPSIA Compliance Information: Batch #CSPK19 For further information contact Rosen Publishing, New York, New York at 1-800-237-9932.

Contents

Being a Kid

It's not easy being a kid. Your parents always tell you what to do. "Finish your homework. Eat your vegetables. Don't talk to strangers. Now go to bed!" Your parents are **responsible** for taking care of you. They tell you these things because they love you and want you to grow into a happy, healthy adult.

4

The Parent in Your Life

Some kids live with their mom and dad. Some live with one parent and visit the other. Some kids live with other family members, such as grandparents or aunts and uncles. Others have foster parents or **guardians**. All kids need a parent or responsible adult to take care of them.

Keeping You Healthy

Parents want to keep you from getting sick. If it's cold, they'll say, "Wear a coat!" They'll put sunscreen on you in summer so you don't get sunburned. Parents make you eat fruits and vegetables to keep your body strong. They tell you to go outside and play so you'll get exercise.

Staying Safe

Everyone knows accidents happen, and parents want to keep you safe. They tell you to look both ways before crossing the street. They remind you to buckle your seat belt in the car and wear your helmet while riding a bike. Parents also tell you not to talk to strangers.

Rules in Schools

All parents want their kids to be happy and **successful** when they grow up. That's why parents send their kids to school every day. Parents tell their kids to listen to other important leaders at school—teachers! Parents also help kids with homework and help them study for tests.

Thinking of Others

Parents teach us how to treat other people. They teach kids to say please and thank you. Parents want to make sure kids are **considerate** of other people's feelings. You shouldn't say things that could hurt someone. When you're nice to people, they will be nice to you too.

15

Telling the Truth

Let's say you broke your mom's favorite lamp, and you're scared you'll get in trouble. Lying might keep you out of trouble for a little while. But your parent would tell you that it's always better to tell the truth. You'll feel better and your parent will know that they can **trust** you.

Making Mistakes

Nobody's perfect. When you make a mistake, bad things might happen. Your parents will help you learn from your mistakes. They'll show you what went wrong and how to fix it. They may tell you that sometimes mistakes lead to good things. Chocolate chip cookies were invented by mistake!

19

I Can't Hear You!

Sometimes it's hard to do what your parents say. You may feel like you should be able to do whatever you want. But your parents have good reasons for telling you what to do. They were kids once too! They have more **experience** and can give you **advice** to help make you a better person.

Lessons from Love

Parents tell kids what to do because they love them. They want to teach you how to take care of yourself. They want you to be kind to other people. They want you to be happy and strong. If you listen to your parents, you'll be the best that you can be!

Glossary

advice: A suggestion about something.

considerate: Thinking of other people's feelings.

experience: Knowing about something after doing it.

guardian: Someone who is in charge of taking care of someone else.

responsible: Being the person who takes control of something and makes sure it gets done.

successful: To have finished something with a good result.

trust: The belief that another person is telling the truth.

Index

Websites

Due to the changing nature of Internet links, PowerKids Press has developed an online list of websites related to the subject of this book. This site is updated regularly. Please use this link to access the list: www.powerkidslinks.com/ltl/parents